HOLOCAUST BIOGRAPHIES

Elie Wiesel
Spokesman for Remembrance

Ellington Middle School
Library Media Center

Dr. Linda Bayer

THE ROSEN PUBLISHING GROUP, INC.
NEW YORK

The author wishes to dedicate this book to Grace Stern,
whose compassion, insight, and sense of justice are
as profound as they are rare.

Published in 2000 by The Rosen Publishing Group, Inc.
29 East 21st Street, New York, NY 10010

First Edition

Permission to use excerpts from *All Rivers Run to the Sea* and
Night by Elie Wiesel has been granted by Alfred A. Knopf, a
division of Random House, Inc.

Library of Congress Cataloging-in-Publication Data

Bayer, Linda N.
  Elie Wiesel : spokesman for remembrance/ Linda Bayer.—1st ed.
    p.   cm.—(Holocaust biographies)
Includes bibliographical references and index.
Summary: Describes the life of Elie Wiesel, Holocaust survivor,
humanitarian, and recipient of the Nobel Prize.
    ISBN 0-8239-3306-7 (lib. bdg.)
    1. Wiesel, Elie, 1928– —Juvenile literature. 2. Authors,
French—20th century—Biography—Juvenile literature. 3. Jewish
authors—Biography—Juvenile literature. 4. Holocaust survivors—
Biography—Juvenile literature. [1. Wiesel, Elie, 1928– 2. Authors,
French. 3. Holocaust survivors. 4. Holocaust, Jewish (1939–1945).
5. Jews—Biography.] I. Title. II. Series.
    PQ2683.I32 Z56 2000
    813'54—dc21
                                                   00-008567

Manufactured in the United States of America

Contents

This map shows the number of Jews killed in Europe during the Holocaust, by country.

Introduction: "Never Shall I Forget . . ."

Elie Wiesel's journey led him from childhood in the Romanian/Hungarian countryside to achievements on the world stage, where he became a renowned author and teacher, Nobel prize winner, and chairman of the presidential body that planned the U. S. Holocaust Memorial Museum. Before being freed from Buchenwald in 1945, Elie suffered in the concentration camps of Birkenau, Auschwitz, and Buna.

Six million Jewish men, women, and children were slaughtered in what came to be called the Holocaust. Wiesel spent his adult life bearing witness to the nightmare he experienced and the atrocities inflicted upon his people. He wrote, taught, and lectured about this tragedy in hopes that such genocide would never happen again.

Elie Wiesel was just a teenager when the Nazis invaded Hungary during World War II as part of Germany's attempt to conquer all of Europe, if not the entire world. Troops marched into his village of Sighet and forced Jews to wear yellow stars. Among other laws designed to isolate Jews from the rest of the population, edicts were issued forbidding Jewish people from going to school with Gentiles or doing business with non-Jews. Soon, Jews were forced to move into a ghetto located in one crowded section of town. Finally, all the Jews were driven out of Sighet and shipped to concentration camps where most of them were gassed or otherwise murdered.

Elie Wiesel's mother, sister, father, and many friends and relatives were slaughtered in the camps. Ten years after being liberated, Wiesel wrote the following description of his first night in the death camps in his memoir *Night*:

Adolf Hitler, the leader of the Third Reich, was full of hatred and prejudice. Under his leadership, the Nazis followed a racist policy aimed at exterminating all Jews and other people the Germans considered inferior. The Nazis thought of themselves as a master race of supermen, but they were actually mass murderers. In selecting Jews for persecution, the Nazis turned against a biblical people who had given the world the Ten Commandments, including the prohibition "thou shalt not kill."

Never shall I forget that night, the first night in camp, which has turned my life into one long night, seven times cursed and seven times sealed. Never shall I forget that smoke. Never shall I forget the little faces of the children, whose bodies I saw turned into wreaths of smoke beneath a silent blue sky.

Never shall I forget those flames which consumed my faith forever. Never shall I forget that nocturnal silence which deprived me, for all eternity, of the desire to live. Never shall I forget those

moments which murdered my God and
my soul and turned my dreams to dust.
Never shall I forget these things, even if I
am condemned to live as long as God
Himself. Never.

More than any other writer—with the
possible exception of child author Anne Frank,
whose diary was published after her death in a
concentration camp—Elie Wiesel brought the
Holocaust to world consciousness. He fought
against bigots who sought to deny that this
tragedy—also called the *Shoah*—ever
happened. Wiesel is often called upon when
moral issues are at stake. He travels throughout
the world and works to prevent bigotry and
other forms of discrimination from claiming
future victims. In this book you will learn about
his struggles and triumphs.

1. Childhood in the Bosom of Family

Elie Wiesel was a middle child—and the only son—in a family of two older sisters, Hilda and Bea, and a younger sister, Tsiporah, listed as "Judith" on her birth certificate. (Even before the Nazis invaded with all their anti-Semitic laws, the Romanian authorities refused to permit certain Jewish names.) Elie's parents, Shlomo Wiesel and Sarah Feig, married out of love at a time when arranged marriages among young people—who often had never met one another—were the norm. Matchmakers or parents usually selected a bride for a boy. Elie had been told that his father caught sight of a woman in a carriage and was struck by her beauty. This girl was the youngest daughter of *Reb* (Rabbi) Dodye Feig from the village of

Bichkev. The following year, the young couple's wedding took place.

Elie was born in 1928 and named after his grandfather, Eliezer, who had been killed during World War I while working as a stretcher-bearer not far from the village where the Wiesels lived. Shlomo Wiesel, a leader in his community, was widely respected for his wisdom and common sense.

A Serious Child

Elie was a serious, shy, sickly child who preferred books to sports. Chess was the one game he enjoyed, and he never learned to swim. A thin, thoughtful boy, Elie loved his little sister, whom he later described as a "golden-haired angel." Intimidated by classmates at an early age, Elie often feigned illness so he could stay home with the mother he adored.

An insecure youngster, Elie tried to bribe his classmates with fruit, buttered bread, and other snacks in hopes of winning their affection. Later he offered presents and even money taken from the till at his father's store. Still, the children scorned Elie, who remained somewhat apart.

Finding Solace in Religion

On Friday nights and Saturdays, however, Elie loved being at home with his family, singing songs around the festive table. Six days a week, his father worked at the small grocery store he owned. *Shabbat* was the one time during the week when Elie spent time with his father, who often invited dinner guests—especially beggars and other poor souls unable to afford good food—to celebrate the Sabbath.

On the seventh day, according to the Bible, God rested from all His work creating the earth. Observant Jews follow Sabbath laws that prohibit all forms of work on this day. Instead, eating, praying in synagogue, studying religious texts, and relaxing are prescribed activities. As Elie grew older, he continued to enjoy the Sabbath and practice all its rituals.

At eight years of age, Elie accompanied his mother—as he
did every year—to seek a blessing of health and well-
being from Rabbi Israel of Wizhnitz, who had come to
visit Sighet. After asking Elie to sit on his lap and review
the lessons the boy was learning in *heder* (religious
school), the rabbi asked Elie to leave the room while he
imparted a special message to the boy's mother. Sarah
Wiesel began sobbing. Elie thought he must have said
something wrong about his studies. Only decades later
did Elie accidentally learn, from a relative who was there
that day, what news the rabbi relayed to the distraught
mother. "Sarah, I know your son will become a *gadol
b'Yisrael* [great man in Israel], but neither you nor I will
live to see the day." (from *All Rivers Run to the Sea*)

Elie became increasingly more religious in
the years following his *bar mitzvah*—a
religious rite of passage marking a Jewish boy's
entry into manhood at age thirteen. The
youngster's maturation is celebrated in
synagogue by his chanting aloud in Hebrew
before the congregation and saying blessings
over the Torah scrolls containing the Five
Books of Moses.

War Coming

In 1943, as the war grew closer, life began to change for the Wiesels. They no longer went away on holiday. On Saturday afternoons in spring, Elie used to go for walks in the Malompark or along the banks of the Tisza and Iza, his town's two rivers. Years later he recalled an acrobat performing there on stilts

Elie Wiesel spent his childhood in the village of
Sighet in the Romanian countryside.

and a tightrope walker who fell, to the crowd's horror.

As with the tightrope walker, the peaceful way of life for Jews in Sighet was in peril and about to fall. The outside world was growing increasingly dangerous. Soon the effects of anti-Semitism in Europe would change Elie's life forever.

2. Anti-Semitism in Sighet

Sighet was the capital of a region of Romania, which from 1940 to 1947 was briefly part of Hungary. In 1640, Jewish refugees started settling in Sighet to escape from persecution in other countries. By 1690, the local population demanded that Jews be expelled from the entire area, but the authorities resisted this bigotry.

Despite official tolerance, the growth of anti-Semitism in Sighet and other parts of Europe paved the way for the Holocaust. In Wiesel's memoirs, he writes of Gentile friends in Sighet wearing masks and horns while carrying whips on Christmas Eve and taking part in a vicious hunt for Jews. Sadly, Elie came to expect anti-Jewish hatred. From the beginning, he saw that the problem belonged to the persecutors, not the victims.

Looking for Answers

As the situation grew worse for Jews in Sighet, Elie could no longer afford to ignore what he saw and began asking why his Christian neighbors behaved so badly. Elie's teachers responded by reciting the history of Jewish persecution dating back to the biblical patriarch Abraham. "Better to be among the victims than the killers," Elie learned from the Talmud.

Elie became increasingly frightened by the rise of the Iron Guard and its anti-Semitic agenda. Slogans like "Jews to Palestine" (meaning: "Jews get out of here") began to appear on the walls of Elie's town. On days that were particularly dangerous, Elie's father told his children to stay home from *heder*. The Wiesels would bolt shut the door to their store and escort regular customers through their living room and then into the back of the store. (The Wiesels lived in a one-story brick house on a corner lot. Their living quarters were attached to the grocery, where Grandma Nissel used to help out on market days.)

16

As anti-Semitism grew in Europe, anti-Jewish graffiti began to appear. The slogan above translates as "The Jews Are Bloodsuckers."

During pogroms—periods in which Jews were killed, often with the approval of local authorities—the family hid in the basement. Wiesel's Jewish studies helped fortify him spiritually against this onslaught. He learned about other periods in history when his people's martyrs had the courage to maintain their religious beliefs in the face of persecution.

The World Stage

In the late 1930s, European leaders met with Hitler in Munich and gave the Führer the Czechoslovak region of the Sudetenland. British Prime Minister Neville Chamberlain triumphantly declared that he had bought "peace in our time." In truth, this policy had the effect of abandoning Czechoslovakia, a

British Prime Minister Neville Chamberlain made a deal with Hitler, seeking "peace in our time."

democratic country that other free nations were obligated to protect.

Furthermore, this conference at Munich marked Hitler's transition from diplomatic maneuvering to outright aggression. Soon, the first refugees from Czechoslovakia began arriving in Sighet. Elie Wiesel was ten years old. Elie barely noticed the *Anschluss*—Germany's absorption of Austria in 1938—or Hitler's invasion of Poland the following year.

Only a boy, Elie paid little attention to the Nuremberg Laws that were enacted, stripping German Jews of all rights and discriminating against them in every walk of life. Not being interested in sports, Elie hardly followed the Olympic Games at which Hitler hoped his Aryan supermen would vanquish what he considered inferior races such as Jews, blacks, and Slavs.

Kristallnacht (Night of Broken Glass) was an organized pogrom targeting Jewish shops, homes, and houses of worship. The Wiesels read about this terrible riot that erupted throughout Germany; more than a thousand synagogues

The Nuremberg Laws stripped
German Jews of their rights.

and seven thousand Jewish businesses were burned. Ninety-six Jews were killed, and Jewish cemeteries were looted along with other Jewish property—hospitals, schools, and homes.

The danger seemed remote, however. The Wiesels still hoped the Third Reich would crumble under its own weight or be stopped by the great powers of Europe. Excessive optimism and faith in mankind prevented the Wiesels and other Jews from leaving Europe while they still could.

Still Holding on to Hope

Originally part of Romania, Sighet was annexed—with Nazi approval—by Hungary. Perhaps the Jews of Sighet felt a false sense of security because Hungary, although allied with Germany, initially treated the Jews there as it saw fit. Except for discrimination at the university and major academies, Jews had less cause for complaint than in other parts of Europe. Hungarian Jews were exempt from

Stalin and Hitler redrew the borders of Poland, Hungary, and Romania. The Soviet Union came closer to Sighet. Some Jews, a few of Elie's relatives among them, took the opportunity to slip across the frontier to help build what some believed would be a Communist paradise for workers. Instead, the Jews were imprisoned in an empire of Russian penal camps later called the *Gulag.*

Distant relations of Shlomo Wiesel were arrested immediately upon setting foot on Soviet soil. Leizer Bash and his fiancée were charged with "spying for bourgeois fascists" and spent more than ten years behind bars in Siberia. Leizer was a Yiddish writer who described his experiences in the *Gulag* a decade before Alexander Solzhenitsyn wrote his monumental work on this topic.

Germany continued to invade other European countries—the Netherlands, Belgium, and Luxembourg. News of massacres in Poland began to reach Sighet. In 1941, more than a thousand "foreign Jews" (those unable to document Hungarian citizenship) were expelled from Hungary to Polish Galicia.

One person from this group, Moshe the beadle (sexton), managed to escape this expulsion and return to Sighet. Dazed, Moshe told his fellow townsfolk that the "foreign Jews" had been slaughtered and buried naked in ditches near Kolomyya, Stanislav, and Kamenets-Podolski.

He described the brutality of the killers and the agony of children and old people, some of whom had been only wounded and therefore died slowly after being buried alive. The desperate witness was considered mad. Few of the Jews heeded his warning to leave Sighet.

Moshe the beadle was one of the characters who later appeared in Wiesel's writing about this period in his life. When Elie subsequently asked his father if the family could go to Palestine, the senior Wiesel responded that he was too old to start over in a new country. Mr. Wiesel would not have offered this response had he known about the Final Solution to the so-called Jewish problem: the attempted extermination of every Jewish person regardless of age, profession, practice, belief, or political orientation.

military service, for example. Young Jewish males were drafted into an auxiliary force that accompanied the troops as quartermasters and dug antitank trenches or cut wood. In Hungary, synagogues were packed, as were Jewish elementary and secondary schools. *Yeshivas* (Jewish religious schools of higher education) flourished. Jewish commerce was booming, as were Jewish cultural centers, sports clubs, and Zionist organizations. Jewish seminars, field trips, and debates could be held openly and legally.

The Jews failed to become sufficiently concerned when Paris fell to the Nazis, Germany won victories in North Africa, and the Japanese bombed Pearl Harbor. The Wiesels followed these developments by listening to Radio London and broadcasts from Moscow. Italian troops passed through Sighet on the way to the front. Jewish refugees from Poland arrived in search of money and false papers so the gendarmes wouldn't expel them.

Elie Wiesel's father worked hard to help these people. The situation gradually grew worse, but the Jews of Sighet—and of many small towns and cities across Europe—couldn't imagine the horror that awaited them. Some families did leave for America, Palestine, England, South Africa, or even China while immigration was still possible. Most waited until the doors locked behind them, and the only way out was to go up in smoke.

3. Mounting Danger

As the laws against Jews became stricter, Shlomo Wiesel discovered that he could help Polish Jews reach Budapest, and not be sent back to Poland, by supplying the refugees with a few American dollars, Swiss francs, or British pounds. Anyone caught with foreign currency was automatically sent to the counterespionage bureau in Budapest. There, an underground network could help them. Almost all Jews who took that route survived.

Elie's father also bribed officials so that Polish Jews could evade arrest and deportation —even though Elie's father didn't know what awaited Jews who were deported. One man whom Shlomo aided was arrested in a raid and tortured. In the refugee's confession, he named

Elie's father as one of the people who assisted him. Consequently, Shlomo was arrested. He spent weeks in prison, first in Sighet and later Debrecen. Thanks to friends in Budapest who were able to pay off either the prosecutor or the judge, Elie's father was released.

As the Germans advanced, Elie Wiesel retreated further into the world of religion, where he contemplated the nature of God. One of his teachers, Kalman the Kabalist, advised that Hitler should be resisted through piety and prayer.

During this turbulent time, Elie was having a stormy adolescence. He was still insecure, prone to outbursts of jealousy and anger if two of his peers became too close. Sometimes he stayed awake all night, feeling rejected. However, Elie also developed strong bonds of friendship. Itzu Goldblatt and Elie competed over everything religious—even who would be the first to see the Prophet Elijah in his dreams. Itzu gave Elie his initial lesson in English, the language of what would one day become Elie's adopted country.

A Terrible Turn

On Sunday, March 19, 1944, Elie was in the House of Study reciting prayers. It was two days before the celebration of Purim, which commemorates the exploits of another tyrant—Haman—who sought to destroy the Jews in ancient Persia. Suddenly, a man interrupted the religious service to report that the Germans had crossed the border and were occupying the country.

Although everyone agreed that this news was terrible, few foresaw what lay ahead. Even though the Red Army was making headway against Germany, the Allied invasion at Normandy would take place soon, and Adolf Hitler's Third Reich was essentially doomed, no one warned the Jews of Sighet or tried to save yet another community slated for annihilation. Berlin needed every train for the war effort, yet railcars were diverted to take Jews to concentration camps. Hitler's "war against the Jews" took priority over his fight against the Allied forces.

Uprising

The Warsaw Ghetto uprising took place in the spring of 1943. Between July and September of the previous year, approximately 300,000 Jews had been shipped from Warsaw, Poland, to the death camp of Treblinka. Only 50,000 Jews were left in the ghetto.

In April of 1943, the remaining Jews rose up and fought against the Nazis. The Germans had planned to liquidate the ghetto in three days, but the underground fighters held out for nearly a month. With virtually no training and a limited number of guns, rifles, and explosives, these Jewish men and women fought longer than the French army against the might of heavily armed German forces. This historic uprising took place nearly a year before Sighet was invaded.

The Nyilas, or local fascists, began preying on Jews with increased ferocity. They threw Jewish students from moving trains and attacked Jewish women. The government in Budapest issued decrees closing Jewish stores and forbidding Jews from leaving home except during certain hours. Jewish state employees were fired. Jews were no longer allowed to walk

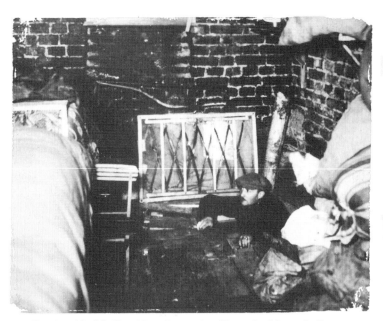

In April 1943, the Jews in the ghetto of Warsaw, Poland, rose up to fight against the Nazis.

in municipal parks; go to the movies; or take buses, trams, and trains.

A few days before Passover, the holiday commemorating the Israelites' escape from slavery in ancient Egypt, German troops in black uniforms arrived in Sighet. Tanks, jeeps, and motorcycles rolled through the streets. On the seventh day of Passover, which traditionally symbolized the miraculous crossing of the Red

Sea, a series of new decrees were issued. The town crier, a hunchback carrying a drum that was too big for him, announced the bad news. (The synagogues had already been shut down.) All offices belonging to Jews were closed. Jews were allowed to leave home only in the late afternoon to buy food.

Darkness in Sighet

Shlomo Wiesel was technically no longer allowed to sell anything, but the shelves in his store were soon empty. Elie's father gave customers whatever they wanted, whether or not they paid. Elie and his sisters helped.

Three days of curfew followed. All Jews had to sew yellow Stars of David onto their clothing as a form of identification. Elie wore his proudly, feeling that this insignia connected him to the Jews of the Middle Ages and other periods of persecution.

Posters, signed by the German military governor, suddenly appeared on walls. These

When a curfew was imposed in Sighet and
elsewhere, the Jews were forced to wear yellow
stars on their clothing as identification.

signs warned that anyone who opposed the new world order would be shot. Special units of the army and gendarmerie began raiding Jewish homes. Inspections and searches were conducted. Jews were threatened. All jewelry, silver, gold, precious stones, foreign currency, and objects of value belonging to Jews had to be surrendered. Anyone who resisted was beaten by the soldiers. Elie's father tried to joke about the situation: "The only thing they'll find in most Jewish homes is poverty. I hope they confiscate that, too." Even poor families often had silver candlesticks or Kiddush cups (for blessing ritual wine on the Sabbath). Many Jews tried to hide these heirlooms in cellars or attics.

The Hungarians carried out Adolf Eichmann's orders with great cruelty. They trampled on old people and the sick, attacked women and children. The Jews were practically relieved when the announcement came that they would be segregated into a ghetto—away from the sadists.

Once again, Elie felt as though he were reliving a page in medieval history. Jews were crowded into poor sections of town as their ancestors had been in Italy, Spain, and then Germany and Poland. When Elie looked up the word "ghetto" in his mother's cherished possession, the *Jewish Encyclopedia*, he was surprised to learn that in Rome, Alexandria, and Antioch, in the old days, Jewish quarters were created *by Jews* who feared alien influences. Only later were ghettos imposed on Jewish residents by prejudiced rulers. In 1480, the Spanish Catholic monarchs Ferdinand and Isabella issued an order consigning Jews to ghettos. Likewise, in 1555, Pope Paul IV drove Jews out of all his cities (except those who lived in the ghettos).

Around the time the ghetto was formed in Sighet, Maria—the Wiesels' Christian house-keeper who had worked for the family since Elie was born—offered to hide her employers at her cabin in a remote mountain hamlet. This kind-hearted peasant woman assured the Wiesels

that there was room for everyone, including
Grandma Nissel. Maria begged the Wiesels to go,
insisting she would bring all food and
provisions. Like the famous Frank family, the
Wiesels might have hidden from the Nazis
during the war. However, without information
about the death camps, Shlomo Wiesel didn't
realize that he needed to save his family—not
just from hardship, but from murder.

The failure to see the Nazis for what they
were is a psychology lesson about the power
of denial. After all, Adolf Hitler spelled out the
plan to exterminate the Jews in *Mein Kampf
(My Struggle)*, written in 1924 and published
in translation in 1940. Even if the Wiesels
hadn't read the book, why didn't anyone else
explain it? Journalists, leaders, historians, or
policy analysts could have warned the Jews.
The first reaction to fatal illness or death is
often denial. Likewise, European Jewry
blocked from consciousness clues about their
perilous plight.

4. Night Descends: Deportation

Elie's family didn't have to leave home to move into the ghetto because their house on Serpent Street happened to fall within the boundaries of the designated Jewish quarter. (In addition, a smaller ghetto was located across town.) The Wiesels kept the largest room in the house for themselves, and relatives crammed into other parts of the modest-sized home.

Most Jews in Sighet were forced to give up everything they had accumulated over a lifetime. There was hardly any space for possessions in the small room or cellar to which a whole family typically was assigned. The Germans also demanded that the ghettos supply a daily battalion of Jewish laborers. Lists were drawn up, and few people avoided the draft. Failing to comply would have put other

Jews at risk, who would be selected to replace the absent workers.

One Saturday in May, about a month after the ghetto had been formed, two high-ranking Gestapo officers arrived at Elie's house. (Afterward, Elie was told that one of the men was Adolf Eichmann, which is why Wiesel thinks he recognized him in Jerusalem many years later at Eichmann's trial.) The Council of the Elders was summoned for an emergency. Transports to expel all Jews from Sighet had been planned. The first convoy was to begin the next morning, but Elie's street was not part of that group.

The Wiesels spent the night helping friends prepare to go. The rumor in the ghetto was that the Jews were being taken to a Hungarian labor camp where families would be allowed to stay together. On May 16, the Wiesels' turn came. "All Jews out!" the soldiers screamed.

The previous night, the Wiesels had dug a dozen holes under trees to hide what remained of their money and precious objects. Elie buried the gold watch he had been given as a *bar mitzvah* present. The family imagined that someday when this nightmare finally ended, everyone would be able to return.

Two decades later, Elie went back to his home—without his parents and little sister.

Parting

On the Tuesday afternoon in 1944 when the Wiesels were driven from their home, the train they were supposed to take wasn't ready to leave. Elie and his family were transferred for several days to the smaller ghetto where the inhabitants had already been expelled. The Wiesels moved into the home of Mendel, Shlomo Wiesel's brother, and his family.

In the house where these relatives had lived, the Wiesels found sacred books scattered across the floor. Someone must have removed the volumes from Uncle Mendel's bag at the last minute. The table was set, and food remained on the plates. The family seemed to have been taken away in the middle of a meal.

Before leaving Uncle Mendel's home, Elie's mother cooked her family's favorite food: *latkes* (potato pancakes). After a few days, the Wiesels were led to the train station where they were loaded into cattle cars. Ever since, Elie Wiesel freezes each time he hears a train whistle.

Years later, Elie learned some of what happened to Uncle Mendel. Another survivor of Romanian-Hungarian origin, who had been in a concentration camp with Elie's uncle, told the story. Mendel's son had stayed with his father one night, and the next day an SS officer shot him in the head when he discovered that the boy was not in his assigned place. The distraught father threw himself on his son's body as if to save him from death. The SS man then shot the father, too.

Wiesel has written that life in the cattle cars spelled the end of his adolescence. The hunger, thirst, heat, and stench were all unbearable. No toilets or provisions for washing were on the trains. Blankets were held up to give people a modicum of privacy while relieving themselves into a pail.

The prisoners ate whatever food they had brought with them: hard-boiled eggs, dried cakes, or fruit. Elie's mother kept repeating to her family: "Stay together at all costs." Someone asked what to do if they were separated. "Then we'll meet again at home as soon as the war is over," Sarah Wiesel replied.

Thus passed the last hours Elie spent with his family. After midnight the train pulled into a station of some type. Through the cracks in the cattle car's slats, Elie saw barbed wire stretching for what seemed like eternity. Pulled to his feet, Elie was pushed toward the door. Barked orders shattered the darkness. The family managed to stay together, as Mrs. Wiesel had instructed. Then a command was issued: "Men to the left! Women to the right!" Wiesel recalls:

> Eight words spoken quietly, indifferently, without emotion. Eight short, simple words. Yet that was the moment when I parted from my mother. I had not had time to think, but already I had felt the

pressure of my father's hand: We were alone. For a part of a second I glimpsed my mother and my sisters moving away to the right. Tsiporah held Mother's hand. I saw them disappear into the distance; my mother was stroking my sister's fair hair, as though to protect her, while I walked on with my father and the

Why?

Wiesel has asked American presidents, generals, and high-ranking Soviet officers why the rail lines leading to the death camp at Auschwitz—or the tracks going to other camps—were never bombed. At that time, Birkenau—a subcamp of Auschwitz—was killing ten thousand Jews a day. Of course, bombed tracks could have been repaired, but the systematic slaughter would have been slowed down by explosives. Countless lives could have been saved. Bombing the tracks would have been a warning to the Germans that Jewish lives mattered.

The United States was bombing I. G. Farben, a petrochemical factory near Auschwitz that employed Jewish slave labor. In fact, one U.S. pilot asked if he could drop the remainder of his explosives on the death factory at Auschwitz in order to halt the mass murders, at least temporarily. Shamefully and inexplicably, this request was denied.

other men. And I did not know that in that place, at that moment, I was parting from my mother and Tsiporah forever. (from *Night*)

In the Barracks

An order was given to form lines. While standing in line, Elie heard one prisoner ask his age and that of his father. Elie replied that he was not yet fifteen, and his father was fifty. The Jewish inmate told Elie to say that he was eighteen and his father forty. The SS guards wouldn't spare people they considered too young or old to work. Another man pointed to the chimney and flames, telling Elie that he and his family would soon be turned to ashes.

Before long, Elie and his father were standing before Josef Mengele, the cruel Nazi doctor known for doing medical research on twins. Mengele froze people alive to study how long it takes the human body to die. He performed other terrible experiments that killed or maimed his victims. This man carried a baton and waived for people to walk one way or the other: to the gas chambers or to barracks where survivors would be worked to death. Elie told Dr. Mengele that he was eighteen and a farmer, not a student. Mengele pointed to the left for both Elie and his father. The new inmates didn't know which way led to life. Someone told Elie and Shlomo they were heading for the crematory.

Wiesel recalls seeing flames leaping from a ditch nearby and then a man delivering a load of babies to be burned in the ditch. Elie could not believe what he saw and thought he was having a nightmare. He decided to throw himself upon the electric wires and die quickly, but just before reaching the pit of flames, the group was told to turn left and walk toward the barracks.

This long building, with some skylights, looked to Elie "like the antechamber of Hell." Inside, the Jews were forced to strip, keeping only their belts and shoes. Guards kept beating the naked prisoners. Next the inmates were taken to the barber, who used clippers to remove all hair from their heads and bodies. Milling around, people greeted friends they recognized despite their changed appearance. Everyone was weeping.

Close to five o'clock in the morning, the *kapos* (guards who were also prisoners) drove the group out of the barracks. Elie and his father were forced to run with the others to another barracks where all the new arrivals were soaked in disinfectant followed by a hot shower. They were made to run to a storage room full of striped, skimpy uniforms. After dressing, the men were ordered to stand for hours in the mud. Finally, an SS officer came and told the prisoners that they were in Auschwitz concentration camp. If anyone didn't work, he would be sent straight to the furnace.

Skilled workers—locksmiths, watchmakers, electricians—were separated from the rest. Elie and his father were sent with the unskilled group to a barracks made of stone. Mr. Wiesel suddenly had to use the toilet. When he asked

Elie Wiesel described Auschwitz as "the antechamber of Hell."

for the lavatory, the Gypsy guard brutally attacked him. Shlomo Wiesel fell to the floor and then crawled back on all fours to his son.

Surrounded by SS with revolvers, machine guns, and police dogs, Elie and his father—among the other prisoners—were soon driven from Birkenau to the main part of Auschwitz. Here the buildings were made of concrete. Elie and Shlomo Wiesel were assigned to block seventeen.

5. At Death's Door in Concentration Camps

The next day, the new prisoners were tattooed with numbers on their left arms. Elie was A-7713. Having been stripped of all signs of personal identity—property, clothing, and even their hair—the Jews now had their names taken from them. The intent was to suppress the people's individuality so it would be easier to treat them as though they were not human beings.

The inmates' numbers were checked repeatedly at roll calls. Military marches were often played. Like the strange sign that hung at the entrance gate to Auschwitz—saying, in German: "Work makes you free"—the music was part of a cruel hoax. The concentration camps were built on lies. In truth, work would not set Jews free; inmates were not identical, numbered things to be counted; and the civilized culture suggested by music was absent from these brutal factories of death.

Each morning, the prisoners were given black coffee. At noon, they got watery soup. In the evening, a little bread with margarine was provided. Throughout the day, Jews were subject to beatings. At nine o'clock in the evening, everyone went to sleep—two people per bunk. At night when the inmates weren't too tired, they sang Hasidic melodies. Most Jews believed the war would end soon. Shlomo Wiesel told his son that the rest of the family had probably been sent to a labor camp. The truth was too hard to bear.

Moved to Buna

After three weeks in Auschwitz, Elie and his father were marched with a group of prisoners to a different camp: Buna. A few other children, ten to twelve years old, were also in this convoy. At both camps, there were daily labor gangs. The most important thing was to avoid the frequent "selections." People chosen at such times were sent to their deaths.

At Buna, Elie's group of prisoners was housed in two tents. For work, Elie and his father counted bolts, bulbs, and small electrical fittings. They also loaded diesel engines onto trains.

When the camp officials discovered that Elie had a gold crown on one of his teeth, he was sent to the camp hospital to have it extracted. Elie said he was sick and asked to postpone the tooth's removal. The dentist, who was selling the gold from teeth, was caught before he had a chance to get Elie's tooth. Later, one of the foremen spotted Elie's gold crown and wanted it. This man finally had a dentist from Warsaw remove it from Elie's mouth with a rusty spoon. Elie agreed to the extraction because the angry foreman was attacking Shlomo Wiesel for his inability to march well. As long as Elie tried to keep the gold tooth, the foreman retaliated against Elie's

The sign over the gate at Auschwitz reads
"Work makes you free" in German—a cruel lie.

father. Another time, Elie was whipped publicly until he fainted. Mr. Wiesel had to stand helplessly and watch his son being tortured.

Elie witnessed many executions in Buna. Men were hung for small infractions like trying to steal soup during an air raid. On one occasion, some *kapos* were thought to have stolen arms, and a young boy who acted as a servant to the condemned was also killed. As always, the prisoners were made to witness the murder. When the child was hanging with his neck in a noose, his body wasn't heavy enough to break his neck or strangle him quickly. The boy struggled between life and death for over half an hour.

Crisis of Spirit

Elie wrote in *Night* and elsewhere about his difficulty retaining belief in God as a benevolent, omnipotent being. If the Master of the universe is good and all-powerful, how could He permit innocent children to be slaughtered? Why didn't God intervene to save His "chosen people"? If the Almighty had some part in this kingdom of darkness, then He must be in league with Hitler as some kind of cosmic sadist.

Wiesel continued to challenge God and accuse Him of silence or indifference. As time passed, even fear gave way to weariness. Living from day to day, hour to hour, was a

The horrors Elie witnessed in Buna made him question his belief in a benevolent God.

struggle in the face of starvation, cold, lack of sleep, and abuse. Once, Shlomo Wiesel was selected for death, and Elie was sent out on work detail thinking his father was being killed that day. However, miracle of miracles, upon returning to the block that night, Elie found his father still alive. Mr. Wiesel had been able to convince the SS that he was healthy enough to perform manual labor.

People in the camps who had something to live for, some source of hope, had a better chance of survival—even though, ultimately, whether one lived or died was usually a matter of chance. Some devout Jews clung to their faith in God. Others, like Elie and his father, lived for one another.

Winter came, and the icy wind cut through the scantily dressed prisoners like a knife. In January, Elie's right foot began to swell from the cold, and he needed an operation to save his toes. The surgery was performed without putting Elie to sleep. He soon passed out from the pain. Recovering in the camp hospital, Elie was able to sleep on sheets again and refrain from work detail. But selections were more frequent in the hospital. Elie had to be careful not to stay there too long, feasting on slightly thicker soup and extra bread.

Quick Decision

Only days after the operation, news spread throughout the camp that the front was drawing closer. The Red Army was approaching Auschwitz. The German authorities therefore decided to evacuate the prisoners. They were to be marched overland to another camp closer to the German heartland. Hospital patients would be left behind.

Suddenly, Elie had a decision to make. Should he try to walk on his foot, which was not yet fully healed, or stay behind at the infirmary? Perhaps he would be liberated by the Russian troops. However, the Germans were unlikely to leave hundreds of witnesses to

testify to the atrocities committed at the camp.
More likely than not, all patients would be shot
and cremated. The camp itself might be
mined. Elie was thinking less about the
prospect of death than separation from his
father. The two had managed to stay together
this far. Elie wanted to remain by his father's
side to help him during what promised to be a
long, brutal trek.

With one shoe in his hand (because it
would not fit over the swollen, bandaged
foot), Elie left the hospital and ran through
the deep snow in search of Shlomo Wiesel.
Father and son did not know what to do, but
they decided to keep together and attempt the
march. "Let's hope we shan't regret it, Eliezer,"
Mr. Wiesel told his son. Elie later learned that
the sick prisoners who stayed behind were
liberated by the invading Russians eight days
after the evacuation.

Elie returned to the hospital for one last
night in the camp. Through frosted panes of
glass, he could see bursts of light from

cannons in the distance. He couldn't sleep because his foot felt like it was burning.

The March

The next day, the prisoners wrapped themselves in blankets and layers of clothing before leaving. At the last minute, block heads forced the inmates to scrub the floors and clean up so the liberating army would know "there were men living here, not pigs." When the six o'clock evening bell rang, hundreds of armed SS men—with searchlights and sheepdogs—began marching the prisoners out of Buna. The snow kept falling relentlessly. Elie and his father waited for fifty-six blocks to pass before block fifty-seven was summoned.

Elie had only two pieces of bread tucked in his pocket for the journey. The SS forced the prisoners to run. Anyone who couldn't keep up was shot. The guards screamed curses at the Jews in the frigid darkness. Elie felt as though his body and self were two separate entities. The pain in his foot was enormous. Sometimes, Elie managed to fall asleep while running.

At last, the morning star appeared in a gray sky. The commandant announced that the great wave of people had covered scores of miles since leaving the camp. The prisoners passed through a deserted village. At last, the order came to rest. Exhausted Jews sunk down in the snow. Elie joined some other inmates who fell asleep in a broken-down brick factory with a collapsed roof. Elie's father soon aroused his son and helped him stand. Prisoners who had been trampled or frozen to death lay in the snow. Father and son went to another shed to rest.

The next day they kept marching in the falling snow. SS guards on motorcycles drove the prisoners forward. The convoy finally reached Gleiwitz, where everyone rested for three days. The prisoners were given no food or drink. Guards stood at the door to the barracks and prevented the inmates from leaving. The military front was following the group. Gunshots could be heard. The prisoners hoped the Nazis wouldn't have time to evacuate them.

On the third day, a selection was held. Elie's father was sent to the left while Elie was directed to the right. Terrified, Elie chased after his father. An SS man ran to get Elie and bring him back. In the confusion, some people—including Shlomo Wiesel—crossed back to the side of the living. Others were shot amid the chaos. The able-bodied group was marched to a field cut by railroad tracks. They waited for the train to arrive. The men were given a little bread but forbidden to sit. Standing there, the prisoners took out their spoons and ate the snow that had accumulated on their neighbors' backs.

A long train with cattle wagons, which had no roofs, arrived at last. The prisoners were loaded aboard, a hundred men to each car. The train left. Later on, when the train stopped, the dead were thrown out. Mr. Wiesel was mistaken by a grave-digger for one of the

corpses, but Elie slapped his father until Shlomo's eyes opened.

The train ride lasted for ten days. When the train stopped at some stations, German workmen threw a little bread to the starving prisoners who fought one another for the food—to the amusement of workers and spectators. Elie watched sons fight with fathers for a morsel of bread.

A hundred prisoners got into the wagon that brought the men to Buchenwald concentration camp. Only a dozen arrived alive—including Elie and his father.

Another Parting

Shortly after arriving at Buchenwald, Shlomo Wiesel developed a high fever. Elie felt responsible because, just before an air raid, he had been unable to convince his father to get up from the snow when he collapsed from exhaustion. Mr. Wiesel was simply running out of strength.

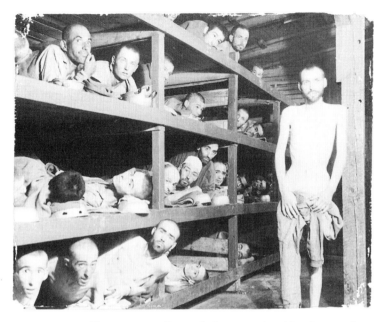

These are slave laborers in the barracks
at Buchenwald. Elie Wiesel is at the far
right of the center bunk.

Elie felt ashamed because he secretly
hoped to be free of the burden his father
represented. Of course, Elie still loved his
father. Much has been written about "survivor guilt"—the fact that innocent victims
tend to blame themselves for surviving a
catastrophe while others were not as lucky.
By contrast, the people actually responsible

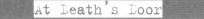

for the tragedy—in this case, the Nazis—may feel no culpability.

Weakened by dysentery, Shlomo tried to tell his son where he had buried money in the cellar back home. For a week, Mr. Wiesel languished. When he begged for water, a guard hit him over the head with a truncheon. Elie climbed into his bunk above his father on January 28, 1945. When the boy awoke on January 29, another invalid was in his father's place. Shlomo Wiesel must have been taken away during the night and brought to the crematory.

6. Orphanage and Education in France

Elie was sixteen years of age when his father, sick and racked by fever, died. The son was overwhelmed with sorrow because he couldn't save his father. After Shlomo Wiesel's death, Elie slipped into a deep state of lethargy that lasted until his liberation on April 11, 1945.

Elie had been transferred to a children's block with six hundred other youngsters. He spent his time in a state of idleness, dreaming about food. On April 5, the camp loudspeaker ordered all prisoners to gather at the assembly place. However, older prisoners whispered to the children that the Germans were going to shoot them. The youngsters therefore refused to report and returned to the block.

An evacuation of the camp soon began, but on April 10 twenty thousand inmates were still in Buchenwald—including several hundred children. When the sirens blew for an alert, the evacuation was postponed. No one had eaten anything—except a bit of grass and potato peels—for six days.

At last, the camp resistance decided to act. Gunfire broke out, and the children stayed flat on the ground in the barracks. The battle didn't last long. The SS fled. Pretty soon, the first American tank pulled up to the gates of Buchenwald. Freedom had come to the survivors.

Freedom and Peril

Three days later, Elie became very ill with food poisoning. He was transferred to the hospital where he spent two weeks hovering between life and death. When Elie was able to stand and look at himself in the mirror, he resembled a corpse. Wiesel explained in *All Rivers Run to the Sea* that although the survivors felt greatly relieved to be safe at last, they "were not happy" and wondered whether they would ever feel joy again. The reign of terror had ended, but for many—like Elie—liberation came too late. He was an orphan, alone in the world, searching for relatives and a place to go.

Lists were circulated with names of people who had survived, but Elie didn't find either of his big sisters' names on these papers. Elie suspected that his mother, baby sister, and grandmother had been murdered. Most survivors were afraid to go back to their hometowns and empty houses. Often, their former residences were now occupied by neighbors who had taken all the possessions left behind. In many cases, survivors who tried to go home were killed by angry Gentiles. Initially, Belgium invited four hundred Jewish youngsters from Buchenwald to move there. However, plans changed when General Charles de Gaulle learned of the children's plight and arranged for them to come to France. Elie was among them.

France—and Reunions

Elie and a few other boys from Sighet went by train from Buchenwald to a boarding school in France, care of the OSE—a children's rescue society. The youngsters were settled in a group home. Leaving Buchenwald aroused mixed feelings for orphans whose parents had been killed in the camps. Many years later,

Child survivors of Buchenwald are escorted out of the main gate by American soldiers. Elie is fourth in the left column.

The OSE, a children's rescue society in France, provided homes for many children who survived the camps.

Wiesel described how difficult it was "to live far from my father, my father who stayed behind, in the invisible cemetery of Buchenwald. I look up at the sky, and there is his grave. When I raise my eyes to heaven, it is his grave I see." (from *All Rivers Run to the Sea*)

At a splendid castle in Ecouis, Elie attended classes and began to return to normal life. He participated in religious services, read books, played chess, sunbathed, hiked in the forest, sang songs around the campfire, and dreamed of going to Palestine. All the children still distrusted strangers and were slow to adjust to the abundance of good food. One day, the headmaster of the school told Elie that his sister had called from Paris and would meet Elie there the next day. Elie was shocked but hopeful. Could his sister have survived? Which sister?

The next day Elie, who spoke no French yet, traveled alone to Gare Saint-Lazare. There on the platform he found Hilda, along with an Algerian Jew named Fredo who had been deported to the concentration camp at Dachau. Hilda and Fredo were engaged to be married. Elie soon learned that Bea had also survived. She had returned to Sighet looking for Elie. Hilda had heard that Elie was dead, but she later spotted his picture in a newspaper, *Defense de la France*. That's how she had tracked down her brother.

After a wonderful reunion, Elie returned to Ecouis. Many months passed before Bea learned

that Elie was alive. Someone finally told her in
Sighet. Elie and Bea made arrangements to meet
in Antwerp, the city of diamond merchants.
There, the three orphans of Sarah and Shlomo
Wiesel were reunited.

By 1947, the OSE hired a private
tutor—François Wahl—to give Wiesel French
lessons. Elie also found good instructors of
Jewish philosophy, Talmud, and other subjects.
Before long, the students were transferred to
Versailles and a new home called "Our Place."
This institution housed not only children from
Buchenwald but girls and boys who had sur-
vived the German occupation either under false
identities or by hiding with Christian families.

Elie went to Paris as often as possible to see
Hilda and her husband. Bea was still in a D.P.
camp (for displaced persons) in occupied
Germany. Elie wrote to her every week and
visited two or three times. Bea's lungs had been
damaged in the camps, and the United States
consequently denied her a visa to emigrate.
Like thousands of other survivors, she was

considered "undesirable" in the United States but eventually was accepted in Canada.

Elie studied at the Lycée Maimonides, often staying there from Monday to Friday. He won a prize for writing an essay about why he couldn't describe his experiences during the Holocaust. At this time, Elie was painfully shy. He developed crushes on a number of girls and yearned for love.

Progress and Struggle

As Elie's teen years drew to a close, he enrolled at the Sorbonne, where he was quite happy. Elie devoured books, loved fine lectures, and took courses in philosophy and psychology, among other classes at the university. Financially, he struggled to live on a meager sum provided by the OSE. He had ration cards, like everyone else. Elie made a little money tutoring a doctor's son in the Bible and Hebrew.

However, despite the return to a more peaceful life, Elie still became despondent and thought about committing suicide. These feelings would persist for weeks, if not months.

Newspapers fascinated Wiesel, and he always read them—regardless of expense. Increasingly, he followed the news in Palestine and elsewhere in the world. The United Nations voted that Jews had a right to a national homeland in Israel and passed the partition plan of November 29, 1947. An exuberant Wiesel rushed to the Jewish Agency in Paris and tried to join the *Haganah* (an Israeli defense force).

Although he failed to become a soldier, another impulsive act did bear fruit. Elie wrote a patriotic letter about how he wanted to serve the Jewish resistance in Palestine. He mailed the piece to a print shop owned by a leading militant in the Zionist organization led by Vladimir Jabotinsky. That very week Elie was invited to the newspaper's secret editorial headquarters and offered a job as a journalist. He was to receive what seemed like a million-aire's salary: thirty thousand francs a month (compared to a fraction of that amount on which he had been trying to live). Elie was able to afford a room closer to the center of town—an apartment with a sink, in fact. Bursting with energy, he moved into the Hotel de France.

In the office, Elie had to translate stories, which had already been published in Israel, from Hebrew into Yiddish. Unfamiliar with Yiddish grammar or the intricacies of Israeli politics, Elie didn't find this task easy. In time, he would venture forth from the print shop and attend press conferences, public meetings, and demonstrations. After a while, translation and errands gave way to editing and writing. In the meantime, Elie still had much to learn about literature and political science.

7. A Newspaper Reporter in the State of Israel

May 14, 1948, was a great day for Elie Wiesel and the rest of the Jewish people. That Friday afternoon Elie listened to Israel's first prime minister, David Ben-Gurion, read over the radio the Jewish state's Declaration of Independence.

This came after thousands of years of exile. Jews had been expelled from the land of Israel in the time of the ancient Romans and then settled in other countries that never fully accepted them. Prejudice had developed against the Jews, whose religion, culture, and history differed from the majority. The Holocaust was one of the ugly results of intolerance. However, throughout the centuries, Jews never forgot Jerusalem or the

Hebrew language. With the creation of Israel, Jews were able to regain control of their ancestral homeland.

In 1948, the French press dispatched its best reporters to cover the story in the Middle East, but Elie Wiesel remained in Paris working as a copy boy and messenger. At first, Elie lived through Israel's struggle vicariously—applauding the fighting units of the Palmach, for example, which opened the road to Jerusalem when the Arabs attacked the fledgling state, and mourning Israel's surrender of the Old City to the Jordanians.

In June, Elie earned the right to publish a story of his own about Israel. It was a fictional commentary on the tragedy of the *Altalena*—a ship filled with Holocaust survivors, munitions from France, and Jewish fighters from the Irgun and Lehi (separate pre-state armies). Presumably out of fear of a political coup, Jewish members of the Tsahal (Israel's regular army) fired on the ship when it came into Tel Aviv harbor. Many Jews were injured or killed.

Elie was distraught that Jewish brothers should turn against one another, like the biblical Cain and Abel, Isaac and Ishmael, Jacob and Esau, or Judah and Israel. In the piece Wiesel wrote, two brothers found themselves fighting on opposite sides when the *Altalena* was attacked.

To Israel

When Passover came in the spring, Elie started to think about visiting Israel during the summer. With the help of friends, he was able to obtain press credentials and work as a free-lance writer covering the lives of new immigrants to the Jewish state. Elie traveled to Israel with the settlers on a ship called the *Negba*. This first trip to Israel was bittersweet for Elie as he thought about the loved ones who were absent from the thrilling voyage.

Elie crisscrossed Israel from the Galilee to Mount Carmel, from the seashore to the desert. Raised in the mountains, Wiesel found himself mystified by the ocean. To quote the American

poet Emily Dickinson, "Exultation is the going of
. . . inland soul to sea, past the houses, past the
headlands into deep eternity." From Haifa's
window on the Mediterranean Sea to Jerusalem's
view of the Judean desert, Elie loved Israel's
varied topography. Years later in 1967, Wiesel's
book *A Beggar in Jerusalem* revealed some of the
author's impressions of the holy city.

Inner Conflict

Elie extended his summer stay in Israel and
worked for a while as a counselor in a home
for adolescents of Romanian and Bulgarian
origin. Like at the orphanages where Elie
himself had lived in France at Fantana and
Ambloy, life at this youth home included songs
sung around campfires, study of sacred
scripture and Jewish history, and classes
dealing with philosophy and literature.

As the autumn rains arrived, Elie grew de-
pressed and withdrew into himself. In Israel,
Wiesel loved the land and the people—but he

also felt alienated. When interviewing the new *olim* (immigrants), especially Holocaust survivors, he learned that they were treated with mixed emotions in their new country. In particular, some Israelis failed to understand how the European Jews could have allowed themselves to be slaughtered. Years before the erection of Yad Vashem, Israel's memorial museum commemorating the Holocaust, many in Israel found the *Shoah* an embarrassing topic. It seemed to perpetuate an image of the Diaspora Jew (a Jew living outside of Palestine) as weak and vulnerable. By contrast, the new Jewish state sought to project heroic stereotypes of brave settlers in a strong citizen army.

Israelis who scorned Holocaust survivors were not aware of the shameful psychological tendency to blame the victim, rather than the perpetrator, for abuse. This was just one of the mistakes that was made in criticizing European Jewry for not resisting the Nazis. In time, Israel would begin to learn how to

embrace the past as part of its collective identity rather than try to repress it.

In the meantime, a lack of understanding and respect for Holocaust survivors within Israel contributed to Elie's melancholy. Here he was in the land of his dreams, feeling a bit useless. Elie began to miss Paris with its sidewalk cafés, small shops, and strolls along the Seine river. He yearned for his friends back in France as well as the intellectual climate of a country whose love of liberty, equality, and fraternity was appealing.

Returning to Paris and Traveling

Suddenly an idea occurred to Wiesel. Why not become a foreign correspondent in Paris for an Israeli newspaper? Elie made some inquiries and found someone who knew an acquaintance of the editor-in-chief of *Yediot Achronot*—the smallest and poorest daily in Israel. Wiesel arranged a job interview and was hired to write freelance pieces for the paper. Elie soon sailed back to Paris on the *Kedma,* sister ship to the one that had brought him to Israel.

On an overcast day in January of 1950, Elie returned to Paris. He moved back into the Hotel de France on the Rue de Rivoli. Elie was delighted with his first article "from our Paris correspondent"; it was an interview with a diplomat at the Israeli embassy in Paris. Soon Elie penned a piece on Beethoven for another publication. Wiesel later wrote about this period in his life in the novel *The Town Beyond the Wall.* A vociferous reader, Elie continued his education by immersing himself in the works of Jean Paul Sartre, Franz Kafka, William Faulkner, and Miguel de Cervantes, among other literary giants.

Before long, Elie made his second trip to Israel. Amid the editorial team at *Yediot Achronot,* Elie was the youngest. In the upcoming years, Elie traveled quite a bit as a journalist—not just throughout Israel but to Morocco (with an official from the Jewish Agency), Spain, and elsewhere.

Elie learned about the visual arts, marveling at the paintings of Goya and Velazquez in the Prado. He visited the hilltop town of Toledo with its beautiful old synagogue that had been converted into a church after the Jews were expelled from Spain in 1492. Elie saw the underground tunnel where Jews could escape to the sea if priests broke into the building. El Greco, another famous Spanish painter, had lived in this former synagogue. Wiesel met with the remnants of Jewish communities wherever he travelled. He even went to Germany and spent a terrible day at Dachau concentration camp.

Back in Paris, Elie was asked by the Israeli paper for which he wrote to prepare a biweekly column called "Sparks from the City of Lights." For a modest monthly salary of twenty-four thousand francs, Wiesel recounted amusing anecdotes, gossip, and stories from the world of arts and letters. He attended museum and theater openings along with various receptions. Elie was hired to work as a translator at the World Jewish Congress in Geneva, Switzerland. At a time when Wiesel had been making the equivalent of only fifty dollars a month, he was suddenly offered two hundred dollars a day. With four months' salary being paid for just a day's work, plus expenses, Elie thought he was a millionaire.

During these years, violent migraine headaches continued to plague Wiesel. Although some studies have indicated that

Elie covered the first negotiations between West Germany and Israel in 1952. Germany agreed to pay reparations to Jews for stealing their property and possessions, depriving them of freedom, forcing them to work as slave labor, and murdering their relatives. Elie opposed these payments for fear that they would be misunderstood and thought to lift blame from the Nazis or place an acceptable price on human life. Wiesel did not want a premature accord to be struck between Germany and the Jewish state. Elie realized, however, that this money helped build the state of Israel and assisted indigent Jews. The alternative—that Germany wouldn't even be held accountable economically for what it did to the Jews—was not appealing either.

migraines—caused by vascular constriction and expansion of blood vessels serving the brain—are more common among geniuses, stress is also a factor in precipitating attacks.

Unresolved memories from concentration camps, combat, or other terrifying incidents—sometimes termed post-traumatic stress disorder—typically haunt victims many years, or even decades, after the threat has passed. Only then is it psychologically safe enough for a person to face some of the most fearful experiences. Subconsciously if not overtly, Elie still lived within the nightmare of the Holocaust, which was not so much behind him as within him.

8. Marriage, Fatherhood, and Writing in America

Over the years, Wiesel continued to travel extensively. In India, he studied the meaning of suffering within the Hindu tradition. In Montreal, Elie visited his sister Bea, who had begun working at the Israeli consulate after settling in Canada with her husband and two children. During a voyage to Brazil on a ship called *Le Provence*, Wiesel spent most of the trans-Atlantic crossing in his cabin, working on a Yiddish account of his time in the concentration camps.

After a ten-year vow of silence, Wiesel had begun the work that became a forerunner to his first memoir, *Night*. When this was first submitted to a publisher, Wiesel was told that no one was interested in the death camps anymore, and that his book wouldn't sell. However, Editions de Minuit agreed to publish the book in French under the title *La Nuit*. This slim, heartbreaking volume did more to bring the Holocaust to world consciousness than nearly any other work ever written.

"To write is to plumb the unfathomable depths of being," Wiesel explains. *Night* came out in the United States in 1960. Worldwide, the reviews were quite favorable. *Night* later became the first work in a trilogy that included *Dawn* and *Day* (*The Accident* in English).

After some time in Israel, Wiesel came to the United States. He planned to stay for just one year, but ultimately remained until his marriage in 1969.

Twist of Fate

In America, Wiesel kept writing and meeting world leaders. In 1956, Elie met David Ben-Gurion when he was assigned to cover the Israeli prime minister's visit with President Dwight Eisenhower. One day in July of 1956 when Wiesel was crossing Seventh Avenue and Forty-fifth Street, he was hit by a taxi. The cab threw Wiesel all the way to Forty-fourth Street, where he lay in the road for twenty minutes until an ambulance came. The first hospital to which the patient was taken refused to accept Wiesel because he had no insurance and very little money. A future Nobel prize winner was almost allowed to die in America because he wasn't important enough.

An orthopedic surgeon on duty at New York Hospital decided to admit Elie and saved his life. The entire left side of Wiesel's body had been shattered. He was put in a cast from neck to foot. Elie could not avoid confronting the irony of having survived the death camps only to be run down on the streets of New York. Wiesel's novel *The Accident* later drew upon some of his experiences recuperating. However, in this book the accident was painted as a veiled suicide attempt. Demons from the past continued to haunt Wiesel.

Hope

In following years Elie became an American citizen and wrote for the *Jewish Daily Forward*, for which he covered the Eichmann trial in Jerusalem. In the mid-1960s, Elie met a young mother of Austrian descent who was in the process of getting a divorce. Marion spoke at least five languages and had studied acting with one of the most famous drama coaches in New York. Having grown up in Vienna, Marion and her family had fled from the Nazis to Belgium, France, and Switzerland. Elie recalls that Marion knew the works of the writer Thomas Mann better than he did! At an Italian restaurant across the street from the United Nations, where Wiesel often went to cover U.N. stories, Elie began falling in love with the beautiful woman who later became his translator and his wife.

On April 2, 1969, in the Old City of Jerusalem, an ancient synagogue—which had been destroyed by Jordan in 1948—was opened for a wedding. Elie and Marion married on the day

Elie admits that he once didn't have enough faith in the future to bring children into the world. His own father's failure to protect his son made Elie fear that he, too, might be inadequate to the task. Marion did not agree. Why give Hitler one more victory? On June 6, 1972, Elisha was born. Named after Elie's father, the infant bore a name that also recalled the child's aging dad.

Jews do not name offspring after the living, so a "junior" wouldn't be acceptable among observant Jews. But perhaps Elie subconsciously acknowledged a part of himself that had died in the choice of his son's name. "Elisha," after all, begins with "Eli." Wiesel says that his son's birth was "a dawn unlike any other." "Because of my father and my son, I choose commitment," Wiesel declares.

before Passover. At forty years of age, the groom looked back on his childhood and adolescence. Was it possible he would marry without his parents at his side? At times of transition in the life cycle, people often return to their roots and review the forces that have shaped them. Despite the love Elie felt for Marion, he was overcome by emotion in the face of so much loss.

When writing *All Rivers Run to the Sea*, Wiesel ended the volume with his marriage. In

Elie, with his wife, Marion, and son, Elisha, after being awarded the Nobel Peace Prize in 1986.

a sense, this act marked the completion of the past and a new beginning for Elie—he was a full adult at last. The title of the second half of Wiesel's autobiography, titled *And the Sea Is Never Full*, quotes the second half of the mournful passage in *Ecclesiastes*: "All rivers run to the sea, and the sea is never full." The names of the two books, like the life they chronicle, form a whole.

85

An Educator and Speaker

Wiesel's works raise painful questions that some people would prefer to forget. Wiesel soon became an educator to convey important but different lessons. Rabbi Yitz Greenberg of the Jewish studies department at City College in New York offered Wiesel a teaching post and the opportunity to give courses in Hasidic texts, Holocaust literature, Jewish studies, and Talmud. Before long, President John Silber of Boston University made Wiesel the Andrew W. Mellon Professor in Humanities.

However, in the mid-1960s, when Yale University approached Wiesel and offered him a position at one of the finest colleges on earth, Wiesel's insecurities got the better of him. "How many *yeshiva* students from Sighet are asked to teach here?" Wiesel thought with pride as well as doubt. Would the time spent preparing for class at an Ivy League school interfere with his writing? Elie remained at Boston University but became a visiting professor at Yale in 1980.

Wiesel was growing from a struggling artist into a symbol of conscience on the world stage. He began speaking out for human rights, wherever people suffer, as well as for the Jewish people. Wiesel traveled to Cambodia in 1980 as part of a delegation to protest atrocities committed by Pol Pot and his Communist Khmer Rouge. Elie went to Nicaragua to meet Miskito Indians expelled from their homes by Daniel Ortega's left-wing regime. The boy who had never learned to swim was now penetrating the jungle in a kayak.

In 1975, Wiesel went to South Africa to oppose apartheid—the racial segregation of blacks from whites by an extremely repressive government. In 1985, in Arizona, Wiesel participated in the first conference to explore possibilities of political asylum for refugees from El Salvador and Guatemala. Wiesel protested terrorism in all forms: against Israelis, through plane hijacking and the massacre of defenseless school children in Maalot; and in Northern Ireland, Sri Lanka, Lebanon, and India.

9. Building a Legacy and a Museum

Among the themes in Wiesel's writing are the conflicts between silence and speech, madness and sanity, indifference and empathy, hope and despair. In dealing with the past, Wiesel explores the relationship between disciples and masters, friends and enemies, resignation and rebellion.

Over the years, Wiesel delivered lectures around the world. He became one of the most gifted, thought-provoking speakers in the Jewish community if not the entire world. People flock to Wiesel's talks. Elie had mixed feelings about his success as a speaker, writing at one point that he even came to loathe the sound of his own voice. In fact, Wiesel's mellifluous voice contributed to the passionate sadness of his message.

Wiesel approaches aspects of the Holocaust as though they are a sacred mystery. He stresses questions, rather than answers, in connection with why this tragedy occurred.

At the White House

In January of 1979, Wiesel came to the White House at Jimmy Carter's request to begin work

Elie at the dedication of the U.S. Holocaust Museum in 1993, with U.S. Holocaust Council chairman Bud Meyerhoff and President Bill Clinton.

as chairman of the President's Commission on the Holocaust. From the beginning, Wiesel had doubts about his role leading an institution that would build a museum to commemorate the Holocaust. Elie did not like fund-raising and distrusted museums as educational tools, preferring books for this purpose.

Despite these reservations, Wiesel lent the prestige of his name to a project that soon promised to erect a major building near the Mall in Washington, DC. A national day of remembrance for Holocaust victims was also established.

On a fact-finding mission for the Holocaust Council, Wiesel led a painful pilgrimage back to Auschwitz. Travel to the Soviet Union on behalf of the museum allowed Wiesel to continue working for Russian Jews. Over the years, the successor body to the President's Commission—the United States Holocaust Memorial Council—hosted a number of international gatherings, such as a Liberators' Conference held in October of 1981 at the State Department.

In 1988, Elie returned to Auschwitz
on a fact-finding mission with
fellow Nobel laureate Lech Walesa.

Wiesel denounced President Ronald Reagan's 1985 visit to a military cemetery at Bitburg where SS officers are buried.

Often, Wiesel's ideals come into conflict with the world. In the beginning of 1985, President Ronald Reagan was scheduled to travel to West Germany. At the urging of Chancellor Helmut Kohl, Reagan decided to visit a military cemetery at Bitburg where SS officers are buried. Wiesel tried to convince the president that honoring Nazi murderers was a bad idea. When Wiesel's efforts behind the scenes proved futile, the writer spoke out against the trip on national television. Elie had been awarded both a Presidential Medal of Freedom and a Congressional Gold Medal. When visiting Reagan at the White House, Wiesel told the president that his "place was with the victims, not the killers." Reagan's visit to Bitburg was one factor that contributed to Wiesel's resignation from the Holocaust Council.

Wiesel was also greatly disturbed by the trivialization of the Holocaust in the media. Following years in which the subject had been largely ignored, a number of television docu-dramas, movies, and popular discussions treated the Holocaust in ways Wiesel considered artistically unworthy or historically inaccurate. Elie said that only victims who were in the camps can understand what happened, while arguing simultaneously for more education about the Holocaust.

A Great Honor

In 1986, Elie Wiesel became the recipient of perhaps the greatest honor in the world. He won a Nobel Peace Prize, which he received in Oslo, Norway. Elie learned that he had been chosen for this award on the afternoon of Yom Kippur, the Jewish Day of Atonement. Marion and Elie started a Foundation for Humanity with the money that is part of the Nobel prize. This institution sponsors conferences on many issues. Some colloquia were devoted to "The Anatomy of Hate"—its causes and cures.

At Boston University, participants studied religious dimensions of hatred and fanaticism. At Haifa University in Israel, the learning of hate was discussed. An international conference of Nobel laureates, which addressed the threats and promises of the twenty-first century, was held in Paris in 1988 on the anniversary of the evacuation of Auschwitz.

Speaking Out

The Wiesels continued to travel extensively. In the spring of 1987, Wiesel testified at the trial of Klaus Barbie—a war criminal who murdered

Elie Wiesel in Oslo, Norway, giving his
acceptance speech after being awarded
the Nobel Peace Prize in 1986.

Jews in Lyon, France. In August of 1988, the Wiesels visited the Jewish community in Australia. In October of 1990, Wiesel visited Russia. The next year he was invited to Romania to commemorate the fiftieth anniversary of the pogrom that took place in June of 1941.

In the spring of 1992, in response to race riots in Brooklyn's Crown Heights, New York Governor Mario Cuomo asked Wiesel to sponsor a conference on ethnic hatred. A seminar titled "To Save Our Children" was held in the autumn. Marion Wiesel worked tirelessly with the governor's staff to plan the event.

In June of 1995, an international conference devoted to "The Leaders of Tomorrow" took

On the eve of the Gulf War, Elie traveled to the Middle East with an old, trusted friend and fellow Holocaust survivor, Sigmund Strochlitz, from Connecticut. At the last minute, Elie canceled a dinner meeting with a cousin in Israel. That night, the home where Wiesel would have eaten was demolished by a Scud missile launched against the Jewish state by Iraq's Saddam Hussein. Wiesel's relatives were unharmed because, in Elie's absence, they went to visit their children.

place in Venice, Italy. Thirty adolescents attended from areas of the world in conflict—the Middle East, Ireland, Yugoslavia, various African countries, and the United States.

In December, a conference on "The Future of Hope" was held at Hiroshima. Ten Nobel laureates, a former Japanese prime minister, Secretary of State Lawrence Eagleburger, several nuclear experts, journalists, and economists all participated. Wiesel went to Belgrade after being asked in July of 1992 to lead a delegation that would investigate prison camps for Bosnians in Serbia. Wiesel met with inmates in an attempt to improve conditions and prevent atrocities.

Seeing how Yugoslavian citizens live in their besieged cities was nearly unbearable. Sarajevo was once an example of urban coexistence. Wiesel asked what went wrong. He spoke out worldwide against Slobodan Milosevic's racist policy of "ethnic cleansing" and supported intervention by NATO (North Atlantic Treaty Organization).

Now

Elie Wiesel has turned seventy. The extraordinary course of this man's life has taken him far from his humble beginnings. Nevertheless, in one sense the writer's heart is still back in his hometown within a Jewish community that no longer exists there. Over Wiesel's desk in New York hangs a single photograph of his home on Serpent Street in Sighet. "When I look up, that is what I see," Wiesel explains. "And it seems to be telling me, 'Do not forget where you came from.'"

Over the years, Wiesel continued to bear witness to the evil forces that destroyed his loved ones and almost all of European Jewry. From all sides, people tried to discourage Wiesel from focusing on the past. A future-oriented America insisted that what no longer exists should be forgotten. True to his heritage and its emphasis on memory, Wiesel remained devoted to a rich tradition. Neither could Elie fail to recall the terrors he experienced in this most violent of all centuries.

Elie Wiesel continues to work for
human rights around the world.

99

Wiesel wrote at the end of his memoir:

> Twilight is approaching, and I know that
> soon it will clasp me into its mysterious
> folds. You [Father] will be there, and you
> will lead me to the others, all those I have
> known and loved. Grandfather Dodye
> and Grandmother Nissel. And mother.
> And Tsiporah. And Bea. And all the
> aunts, the uncles, the cousins, the
> friends. I know that when I shall join
> your ranks, I will hear your voice at last.
> (from *And the Sea Is Never Full*)

As the Talmud teaches, "It is not incumbent upon you to complete a task, but neither are you exempt from beginning."

As much recovery as is possible in a lifetime may have already been achieved by Wiesel. The Holocaust will never disappear from his consciousness; and because of Wiesel's efforts, neither will it disappear from the conscience of the world.

Because of Elie Wiesel's efforts, the
Holocaust will not be forgotten.

Timeline

1933   Hitler is appointed chancellor (prime minister) of the German nation. The first concentration camp opens at Dachau in March. The first laws restricting Jewish rights are passed in April.

1935   The Nuremberg Laws are passed, forbidding mixed marriages between Jews and Christians. Jews lose their rights of citizenship.

1937   The Buchenwald concentration camp opens.

1938   *Kristallnacht* (the Night of Broken Glass) occurs. German mobs destroy Jewish shops and synagogues.

1939   Germany invades Poland in September, beginning World War II. The Auschwitz concentration camp opens.

1940   German Jews ordered to wear yellow stars. Mass deportation of Jews to concentration camps begins.

1941   German Jews sent to ghetto in Lodz, Poland.

1942   Wansee conference is held in January, in which the Final Solution, extermination, is planned for the Jews. The Treblinka death camp is opened.

1944   Allied forces invade Normandy, France.

1945   Russians capture Auschwitz in February; American troops capture Buchenwald and Bergen-Belsen concentration camps in April. Germany surrenders in May.

Glossary

Anschluss
The union of Nazi Germany and Austria in 1938 as
   part of the Axis alliance.

Aryan
In Nazi ideology, a white European Gentile of
   Nordic type (preferably blond and light).

diaspora
The dispersion of Jews outside Israel and
   throughout the world; can also apply to other
   peoples dispersed outside their homeland.

Führer
Leader: the title used by Adolf Hitler as head of
   Nazi Germany; a tyrant.

gendarmerie
Military police with responsibility for public
   security within national territory.

genocide
The systematic killing of an entire ethnic, racial, or
cultural group.

Gestapo
Nazi secret state police started by Hermann
Göring in 1933 to terrorize people.

Gulag
A vast system of prisons in the north of the Soviet
Union where political prisoners were jailed.

Holocaust
The extermination of six million Jews by Nazi
Germany during World War II.

Nazi Party
The National Socialist German Workers' Party
brought to power in 1933 by Adolf Hitler.

pogrom
A massacre of Jews or other minorities, often
sanctioned by local authorities.

Shabbat
Sabbath, on Saturday, when Jews don't work and
celebrate God's seventh day of rest.

Shoah
Word used in Hebrew for the Holocaust.

Talmud
A collection of ancient Rabbinic writings that form
a basis for Jewish law.

theology
The religious study of the nature of God.

Third Reich
The rule of Adolph Hitler and the Nazis in
Germany from 1933 through 1945.

Torah
The Five Books of Moses, or Hebrew Bible, written
by hand on a scroll of parchment.

yeshiva
A religious school for Jewish students, often on the
high school level.

For More
Information

Wiesel, Elie. *King Solomon and His Magic Ring,* with illustrations by Mark Podwal. New York: Greenwillow Books, 1999.

Wiesel, Elie. *Night.* Translated from the French by Stella Rodway. New York: Bantam Books, 1986.

Wiesel, Elie. *A Passover Haggadah,* with illustrations by Mark Podwal. New York: Greenwillow Books, 1999.

FOR ADVANCED READERS

Wiesel, Elie. *All Rivers Run to the Sea; Memoirs.* New York: Alfred A. Knopf, 1995.

Wiesel, Elie. *And the Sea Is Never Full; Memoirs, 1969-.* Translated from the French by Marion Wiesel. New York: Alfred A. Knopf, 1999.

VIDEOS

Spielberg, Steven. *Survivors* (CD-ROM). Hosted by Leonardo DiCaprio and Winona Ryder. Los Angeles: Shoah Foundation, 1999.

Wiesel, Elie. *Passover Seder with Elie Wiesel.* New York: Warner Vision, 1995.

Organizations

Anti-Defamation League, Braun Holocaust Institute
Web site:
   http://www.adl.org/frames/front_braun.html

The Center for Holocaust and Genocide Studies
University of Minnesota
100 Nolte Hall
315 Pillsbury Drive
Minneapolis, MN 55455
Web site: http://www.chgs.umn.edu

Fortunoff Video Archive for Holocaust Testimony
Yale University
P.O. Box 208240
New Haven, CT 06520-8240
(203) 432-1880

The Holocaust History Project
Web site: http://www.holocaust-history.org

Museum of Jewish Heritage:
   A Living Memorial to the Holocaust
1 Battery Park Plaza, 25th Floor
New York, NY 10004-1484
(212) 968-1800
Web site: http://www.mjhnyc.org/home.htm

Simon Wiesenthal Center and Museum of Tolerance
9786 West Pico Boulevard.

Los Angeles, CA 90035
(800) 900-9036
Web site: http://www.wiesenthal.com

Survivors of the Shoah Visual History Foundation
P.O. Box 3168
Los Angeles, CA 90078-3168
(818) 777-4673
Web site: http://www.vhf.org

Terezín Chamber Music Foundation
Astor Station, P.O. Box 206
Boston, MA 0223-0206
(617) 730-8998
(617) 738-1212
Web site: http://www.terezinmusic.org

United States Holocaust Memorial Museum
100 Raoul Wallenberg Place SW
Washington, DC 20024-2150
(202) 488-0400
(202) 488-0406
Web site:http://www.ushmm.org

Yad Vashem Holocaust Memorial,
    Jerusalem, Israel
Web site: http://www.yad-vashem.org.il

Index

Credits

About the Author

Linda Bayer taught high school and completed a Ph.D. in humanities plus clinical training at Harvard University for a second doctorate in education and psychology. Dr. Bayer was on the faculty at Wesleyan University, Boston University, The U.S. Naval Academy, American University, and the Hebrew University. The author of a novel, three nonfiction works, and twelve children's books—including biographies—Bayer was an award-winning reviewer at the *Washington Jewish Week*. She is currently a senior writer and strategic analyst at the White House and mother of a son, Lev, and a daughter, Ilana.

Photo Credits

Cover image © Bernard Gotfryd/Archive Photos. P. 13 © Albert Rosenthal/United States Holocaust Memorial Museum (USHMM); pp. 17, 44 © Yad Vashem Photo Archives/USHMM; pp. 18, 29 © National Archives; p. 20 © Landesbildstelle Baden-Bildarchiv/USHMM; p. 31 © Netherlands Instituut voor Oorlogsdocumentatie; p. 48 © Glowna Komisja Badania Zbrodni Przeciwko Narodowi Polskiemu; p. 64 © USHMM; p. 50 © Archiwum Panstwowego Muzeum w Oswiecimiu-Brzezince/USHMM; pp. 58, 89, 91, 92 © AP/Worldwide; p. 63 © World Wide Photo; p. 85 © Richard Drew/AP/Worldwide; p. 95 © Bjoern Sigurdsuen/AP/Worldwide; p. 99 © Nancy R. Schiff/Archive Photos; p. 101 © Adam Nadel/AP/Worldwide.

Series Design and Layout

Cindy Williamson